THE LOST KEY TO THE SCRIPTURES

by Alvin Boyd Kuhn

©2011 Zuubooks.com. All Rights Reserved. No reproduction of this book may be stored in an electronic device or reprinted without the written consent of the author. United States Copyright and International law applies.

ZuuBooks specialize in offering rare printed and ebooks for affordable prices. For more information on our products and services for authors please contact us at ilifeebooks@gmail.com

ZuuBooks

This has been a ZuuBooks.com Publication. For New and Classic titles in Audiobooks, ebooks, and Paperback please visit us at www.zuuBooks.com

Authors who are interested in publishing and distributing their works can contact us at ilifeebooks@gmail.com

THE LOST KEY TO THE SCRIPTURES

by Alvin Boyd Kuhn

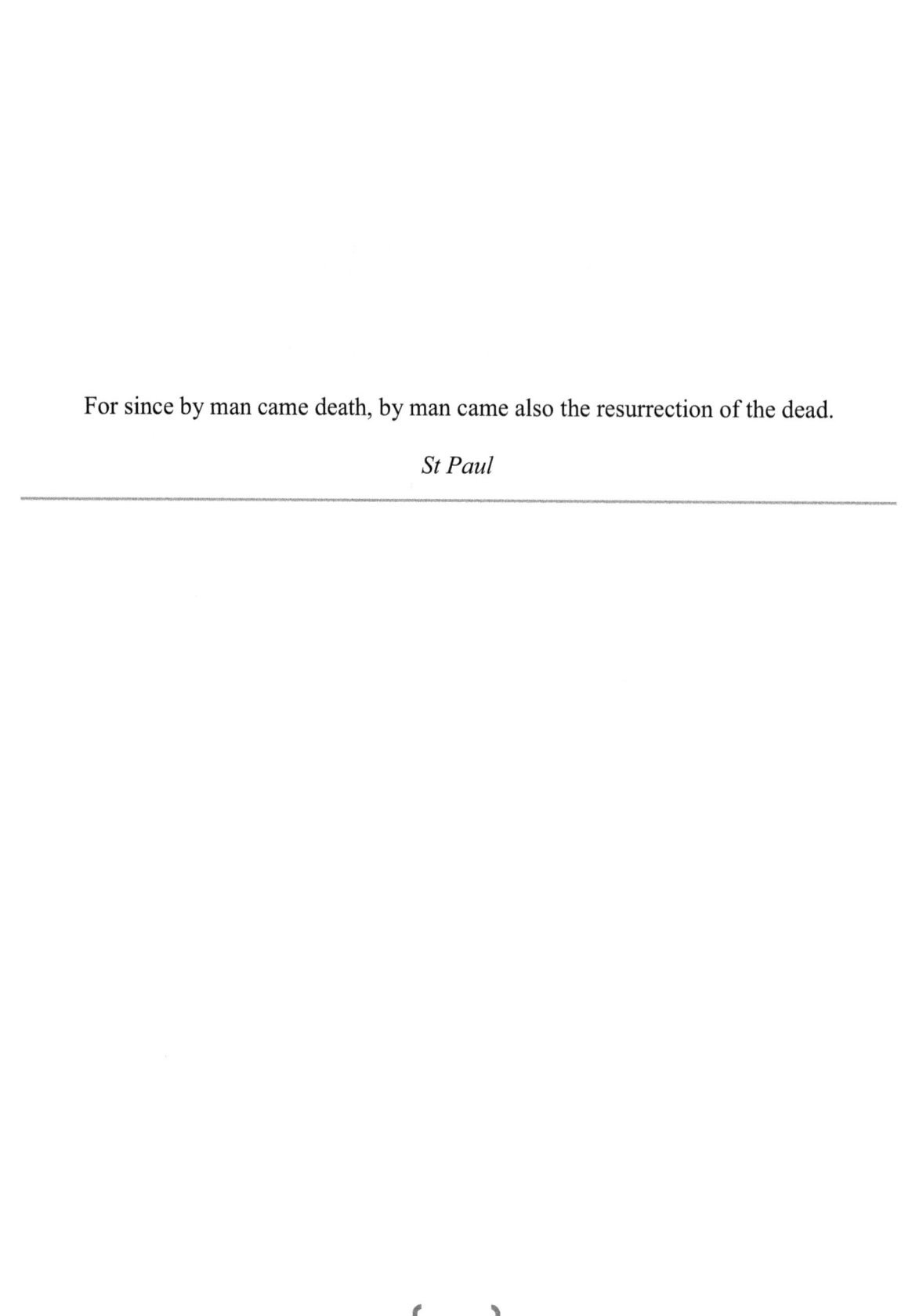

For since by man came death, by man came also the resurrection of the dead.

St Paul

Table of Contents

1	LOST KEYS RECOVERED
2	THREE FATEFUL WORDS
3	RIGHTLY DIVIDING THE WORD
4	THE BODY IS THE TOMB
5	THE SOUL IS DIVINE SEED
6	BREAKING THE BREAD OF LIFE
7	THROUGH DEATH TO LIFE
8	THE VOICE OF ANCIENT PHILOSOPHY
9	SPIRITS IN PRISON
10	THE BOOK OF THE DEAD
11	CHRIST CRUCIFIED IN EGYPT
12	IN THE UNDERWORLD
13	THE TOMB OF THE BODY
14	UNDER THE LAW OF SIN AND DEATH
15	TO HIM THAT OVERCOMETH

Preface

The likelihood of a favourable acceptance of the astounding revelation to be made in this essay will be considerably heightened if the epochal disclosure is preceded by sufficient prefatory exegesis to present it in its proper "frame of reference". So incredible is the true esoteric elucidation of the lost meaning of the Scriptures of Christianity that the immediate reaction will generate the demand to know what historical circumstances or developments could have led in the first place to so fateful a loss of vital knowledge once possessed. It will therefore be judicious to begin the exposition by presenting certain items of the historical background as necessary and highly enlightening introductory matter.

This explanatory material must begin with the broad blunt statement that what is commonly believed about the Bible as a book, its date, authorship and "inspiration", is *all* quite erroneous. Let us be explicit in this: the solid bulk of common belief about this book is totally untrue! There is scarcely a single item of the common man's presuppositions about the Christian Scriptures, — who wrote its books, when it was written, how the composition was "dictated" or "inspired", what its message really means, in what language it was written, what is its assumed historical reference, how and why these particular books were selected out of hundreds to become "the Bible", and other subsidiary questions by the score — that comes within the proverbial mile of the actual truth concerning this mysterious document that for centuries has held the minds of millions under the prodigious obsession of its inviolable sanctity. The grim and sober truth must now be stated, that all general ideas about this volume, disseminated among the masses by the priests of the religions and never corrected by them, are totally, grossly, tragically false to fact.

If this drastic assertion seems to upset the whole apple-cart of conventional ideas on the subject of Bible authorship, the reader will need to brace himself to absorb the next shocking declaration, which undoubtedly will shatter all preconceived notions of the general mind. This jarring blow comes in the blunt statement that, in the common and accepted meaning of the words, the Bible books were never "written" at all! This, it will be said, is self-evident nonsense and folly! A book can't be a book unless it has been written. The retort still is that the statement is sober truth! In the sense in which the word "written" is used today, in reference to a book's authorship, these Bible books never were written. How can this be so? Simply enough, when it is known, *as now it is,* that this collection of documents was in existence for ages and held in the minds of priests and initiates in the ancient Mystery brotherhoods for thousands of years without ever having been committed to writing. They were preserved in memory only. They constituted the body of what is known as the great "oral tradition", a set of ritual formulas, ceremonial rites, allegorical depictions of truth, number graphs and pictorial representations of the realities and phenomena of man's *spiritual* history, that had been transmitted from generation to generation of the hierophants of the ancient religions in unwritten form. Finally here and there, for one reason or another, chiefly lest they be lost or forgotten or too badly corrupted by change, they were set down on paper, and so at last came to the later ages as books, presumably "written" by somebody. And once written, they became subject to the human proclivities of tampering, altering and religious skulduggery of many sorts. That they met with this treatment is not only admitted by the historians of Christianity in its early stages, but is even boasted of by the scribes and some of the Church Fathers, who thus initiated the moral justification of a resort to unholy means for the achievement of "holy" ends. Summing up volumes of history in a sentence, it can be said that the extent to which the flagrant practice of literary forgery was carried in the days of apostolic fervour is well past the belief of those who have not read the massed evidence.

So the books of the Bible were never "written" at all, in the modern understanding of literary authorship. They were not the original lucubrated creation of individual minds producing a written document that had not been in existence before such authorship. They were in large part the final deposit on paper of the sets of ritualistic formulas, dramatic scenarios, allegorical depictions, all representing the aspects of cosmic reality and spiritual truth; and they were often just the transcripts of the lines to be recited by the actors in the great Mystery plays of the ancient religion. Prominent among the material were the choral odes and runes to be chanted in accompaniment to the symbolic religious dances that imitated the rhythms of the universe.

Such has become the "set" of orthodox Christian thinking on such matters that when the statement is made that Scriptural material is not history in the modern sense, but is spiritual allegory and drama of cosmic verities, the reaction is inevitably one of mental let-down in evaluation of the importance of the Holy Word. This is a wrong attitude and must be corrected before another word is put down. Whether the reader is prepared to give credit to the truth of the statement or not, it must be said categorically that not only does the acceptance of the Bible contents as allegory instead of history not diminish their value, but it is the only device that will open the door to any appreciation of their true value. In short it is to be said that the Bible becomes infinitely more significant when taken as allegory than when read as ostensible history. (Unquestionably *some* history was interpolated at a later time, so that it is hard in places to determine where allegory stops and history begins)

The high value of the allegory inheres in the fact that it faithfully portrays to discerning minds the inner core of the *meaning* of all history, for it depicts the one thing that is of central importance to all humans, — the spiritual or evolutionary history of the Sons of God, who are our own souls incarnated in mortal bodies here on earth. The Bible is a collection of archaic dramas and allegories pictorializing the experience and meaning of this mundane life of ours. Compared with these divinely produced representations of the structure, plan and import of man's earthly life, what has all along passed for the "history" of a minor tribe of herdsmen in one particular land less than twenty-five hundred years ago falls into comparative triviality and inconsequence. What was known of old, has been forgotten for centuries and must now be learned again, is that the religious myths of ancient times, formulated by near-divine genius, are infinitely truer than history.

All this will sound to the general orthodox reader like veritable heresy against concreted and consecrated tradition and opinion. But it is a poetic truism that "truth crushed to earth shall rise again". And in this matter the suppressed truth is rapidly rising to dissolve incrusted error.

LOST KEYS RECOVERED

If the Bible is a collection of dramas and allegories of the soul's life in body, the point of next importance concerns their interpretation. Everything of value ultimately hinges on this. And because it was ever of pivotal importance, it was right here that ineptitude, unintelligence and chicanery crept in to ruin the operation of the entire scheme of instruction divinely instituted for human benefit. The loss of the symbolic codes and the consequent failure to grasp the proper interpretation sent the entire structure of ancient sagacity crashing down in tragic wreckage.

The trap that caught ignorance in its snares and led to the fatal decline of intelligence necessary for a true interpretation of Scriptural lore is not hard to locate. It was the strange device that ancient genius employed to release truth to the intelligent and the initiated, while hiding it from the base and vulgar mind. For the Bibles were written in a language the very existence of which has hardly been known since the days of its ancient usage — the language of symbolism.

The glyphs and characters of this ancient language have been undeciphered for twenty centuries or more. Only recently have the first steps been taken toward its recovery and restoration. But already it is seen that through its light the interior true meaning of the Bible and theology leaps into glorious significance and luminous intelligibility, so that the whole volume of divine revelation embodied in the Holy Scriptures is at once redeemed from arrant nonsense to sublime import and value. If this is true in any measurable degree, the announcement becomes the epochal event in two thousand years of Christian history. That it is wholly true there is no longer any sound reason to doubt.

THREE FATEFUL WORDS

The rehabilitation of the lost meaning of the sacred books of old properly begins with the revelation of the cryptic connotation of three words in the Bible whose true interpretation will in a flash work a miracle of re-enlightenment in all minds and will in one vivid moment of new realization transform the entire structure of religion and theology. The whole rationale of religious conception, so far as it is based on the authority of Bible literature, will undergo a complete and astonishing reorientation when the great light released by the proper esoteric sense of these three words is turned upon the mystifying problem of sane exegesis. The discovery of this meaning, hidden for twenty centuries, will inaugurate a new era in all world religion.

And what are these three words that carry such vital significance? They are "the dead", "death", and "to die", In essence they are the one word — "death".

It will fall with a stroke of amazement and incredulity upon minds of limited intelligence to be told that these words can possibly have, or could for twenty-five centuries have had, any other meaning in the Scriptures than the one commonly attached to them. What, it will be asked, can "death" possibly mean other than the demise of the physical person which ensues when the impalpable life energy, or soul, detaches itself from the vehicle of flesh? Who else can be the "dead" but those who have lived in body and are now gone across the great divide? What can "to die" mean if not to undergo the separation of the body and the spirit? Surely there can be concealed no mystery here, no hidden sense that could conceivably elude general intelligence.

Yet it is our obligation to announce, in the face of this universal supposition, that these simple words have all the time borne a connotation different from the one commonly supposed to be their standard and established acceptation. And it becomes our privilege, on the strength of tested scholarship, to proclaim that they bear a meaning not only different from the one generally conceived, but one *precisely opposite* to that universally attributed to them. Incredible as it may seem, when used in their theological reference, these words bear a meaning that at one stroke turns the picture of all exegetical significance almost completely upside down! For "to die" means, for the soul, *to live* here on earth; "death" means the soul's *life* here in the flesh; and "the dead" is a term denoting those *alive* here in the mortal body! Could any assertion appear to be more preposterous? Evidence for these assertions, and plenty of it, the reader will be demanding. As to that, the quantity of evidence available to demonstrate the correctness of the pronouncement is almost limitless.

RIGHTLY DIVIDING THE WORD

It is only necessary to take a few brief texts from the Bible and consider dialectically for a moment the words "die" and "death" as there used, to be made aware in a flash that the common meaning of the words does not and cannot apply, and to realize thence that they must carry some hitherto unsuspected connotation. Let reflection dwell for a moment on this passage: "The soul that sinneth, it shall die". This has been read millions of times and almost certainly never without the belief that it stands as a warning pronounced against sinners, holding the threat of a catastrophic end of life in some dismal way as the consequence of evil-doing. Yet so little is the logical genius of the human mind brought into use in connection with Biblical utterances, being lured astray by pious doctrinal persuasions or lulled to desuetude by indoctrinated hypnotizations, that apparently no one has ever paused a second to reflect on the obvious meaninglessness and emptiness of the passage if the word "die" is here taken in its usual acceptance. No one in all the Christian centuries, it would appear, has stopped long enough to register the immediately obvious reflection that the soul that does *not* sin will die too, since all, both the righteous and the ungodly, alike go down to physical death. It is therefore inane and pointless, in fact quite an outright delusion, to warn the sinners that they shall die, when they well know they shall meet the same fate even if they turn to righteousness. What good is a warning to sinners if it can offer no advantage to sinless life? The sentence of sinners to death is utterly nonsensical if "die" is given its common meaning, and no one has known any other meaning to ascribe to it. As a deterrent against sin it carries no moral force whatever, since an instant's thought sabotages the assumed direful punitive character of the judgment. Sinlessness saves no man from death.

Another Biblical citation runs to the same effect: "The wages of sin is death". Similar reasoning process here yields the same nugatory result. The wages of righteousness and virtue is death also. Godliness gains no advantage over sin. The meaning assumed to lie in these verses turns around on itself, so to say, and destroys whatever logical cogency they are taken to possess. Unless "die" and "death" have some other undiscovered reference, these passages are so much pious froth.

But, if the esoteric claim that the Bible conveys beneath the literal sense of its language a profound recondite meaning is to be sustained, — and only on such grounds can it be saved from ridiculous irrelevance in hundreds of items — then it must be concluded that these statements employ the two words "die" and "death" in some other meaning than the decease of life from mortal body. The release of this meaning from the thraldom of ignorance must rank as a cultural event of the sublimest import.

The great revelation throws in our faces the blunt fact that these significant words carried a cryptic meaning having nothing to do with the demise of fleshly body at the end of a life. They bore a secret meaning which becomes veritably the *true* "key to the Scriptures". When once that profounder sense is recaptured and read back into hundreds of passages in the Bible, the lost light of sound theological understanding will glow again in the human mind after centuries of obscuration.

The basic ground for discovery and comprehension of the crucial meaning of these words is found in the Greek Platonic, Pythagorean, Orphic and Neo-Platonic philosophies, and behind these the more ancient wisdom-knowledge of the Egyptians, who bore the bright torch of religious light in times remote beyond common supposition. Long study and profound reflection upon these primeval systems, framed obviously by the great demigod Seers and Sages of antiquity, are an indispensable requisite to the recapture in full of the mighty strategic import of these key words. It is not asserted here that the true cryptic sense of the words has not at any time in centuries been known, or that the pronouncement here made as to their theological meaning is the first revelation of that meaning. Such as assertion would flout the truth in flagrant fashion. Many students have delved into these early systems of philosophy and have been made familiar enough with the recondite sense in which they are used in the systems mentioned.

What, then, constitutes the momentous revelation proclaimed herein? It is the discovery that this cryptic sense of the words holds and must be applied in a vast field of world thought in which no one ever dreamed that it carried its significance and wielded its crucial import. And this vast field of cultural effort is the religion and theology of Christianity. Apparently not one of the many scholars who since early days have been conversant with the ancient philosophical connotation of these words ever gained a flash of intelligence that would have shown him the absolute necessity of carrying their Egyptian and Greek meanings over into the Jewish and the Christian Scriptures! That the esoteric sense of the words does apply there as the veritable keystone of the arch structure of Christian theological systematism constitutes the epochal modern discovery, perhaps the most momentous made in religion in ages.

True and basic meaning was lost from the three words when Christian theology failed to maintain the sharp distinction made by Greek thought between the two elements of the duality in man's nature, the physical body, or the natural man, on the lower side, and the divine soul, or the Christ-in-us, on the higher level. Had this vital and pivotal distinction been keenly held in its system, Christian exegesis would never have made the capital blunder of associating the words "death", "to die" and "the dead" with the *body* of man, but would have kept them, as did the Greeks, in constant reference to the divine *soul* that comes down out of "heaven" to dwell for seventy years in the flesh of mortal body. On this basis it would have been seen all along that "death" was in their conception that comparative and relative "death" which the *soul* underwent when it made its descent from higher realms of consciousness and took residence in earthly forms. In brief, they would have known that the "death" spoken of was of the *soul* and not of the *body*! The soul, coming here from its own glorious home "above", gave its life that the body might have it. It endured the cross of flesh and matter and suffered "death" that the body might live.

THE BODY IS THE TOMB

If the body was the home of the soul in its condition of "death", then it was the grave, the tomb, the sarcophagus, the sepulcher, the mummy-case of the soul. And so one finds the Sages referring to the physical corpus of man as the prison, the underground dungeon, the pit, the cave and finally the tomb of the soul. This life, they said, was the soul's "death," as, conversely, the soul's free life in the higher worlds was the body's death.

But the modern mind knows no meaning applicable to the word "death" that does not connote actual extinction of life or being. So it is puzzled to understand how the sagacious prophets of old could attribute life to the bodily part of man, that actually does die, while representing as "dead" the spiritual part that never can die. It was this paradoxical dilemma which prevented Christian theology from catching the true import of the Scriptures it took over from antecedent Pagan sources and caused it to pervert their underlying significance into unconscionable literal nonsense.

But life itself is the greatest of all mysteries, even to the creatures enjoying it, and the method that ancient sagacity and understanding took to represent to human thought this aspect of the mystery seemed to reverse the principia of common knowledge. Nearly always does profounder plumbing into the depths of thought upset the structures of common presupposition. So the general mind of Christendom, adjusted by centuries of teaching to the bodily reference of the word "death", will be inclined to think that if such is the position of Greek philosophy, it must be a very illogical philosophy indeed. Counter to this natural reaction we would assert that, so far from being illogical and untrue, it is the only rational view that meets the factuality of the situation involving soul and body in living relationship and that yields correct understanding to the mind. It therefore becomes the primary key to the Scriptures.

What, then, is the nature of this "death" that underlies what we call the very opposite thing — life? The answer is found buried deeply under the abstruse signification of another great item of theology, that of the Christ giving his life for the salvation of man. If a living entity gives up its life so that other being may have it, naturally it loses that which it gives away. It cannot both give it and retain it at the same time. And to lose life is to suffer "death". The Son was sent into the world that the men of the world might through his oblation have life more abundantly. He is pictured as the sacrificial lamb, offering his life to creatures of a lower rank who were linked with the realm of mortality. The Son's giving his life as "a ransom for many" entailed his losing it for himself. Hence came his "death". And this "death" was on the cross, not of wood, but of flesh. For the Logos, of which the Christos was a ray, became flesh and dwelt among us. And at last the true meaning of "death on the cross" comes to light. The incarnation of soul in mortal body is all that this phrase means or ever could mean.

The transaction "on Calvary brow" some nineteen centuries ago is a dramatic representation of purely theological meaning. The Christ-soul is on the cross — of flesh and matter —whenever it is linked to body in incarnation. The ghastly conception of the human race's salvation through the shedding of, shall it be said, two pints of blood from "the wounded side" of a physical man two millennia ago, is resolvable into plain intelligible common sense only when it is understood that the Sons of God, taken collectively as the Son of God, transmitted the dynamic energies of their living essence, symbolized as blood (since the blood in all creatures holds the life principle) to the entities of animal-human stature, that they, thus partaking of more exalted being, might have more abundant life.

THE SOUL IS DIVINE SEED

A clearer view may perhaps be gained if the exposition is conducted through the avenue of the analogy of the planted seed. The seed is in fact one of the most fruitful bases of theological apprehension at every turn. It is so because it is the means which life evolves to carry the potentialities of renewing itself in a new cycle across the gulf of non-existence following the dissolution of its living embodiment. The Son is therefore the divine seed of the Father's life, which, like any seed, must fall into the ground, go to decay and lose its life for the very purpose of regaining it. The seed loses its life in the ground in order that it may have a resurrection in the young sprout.

It is precisely true to say that in the descent of his Sons (or his Son) into earthly existence, God plants the seed of his own life in the personal lives of his human children. This, be it stated, is all that is implied in theology by God's condemning his Sons (Son) to "death" on the cross for the sins of the world.

John has put the solid basis of this theological conception in succinct allegorical form when, using the seed as analogy, he says: "Unless a grain of wheat fall into the ground and *die,* it abideth alone; but if it die, it bringeth forth much fruit". Paul, too, asserts that the seeds of divine life sown for the world must first die. He says that the seed we sow is "bare grain . . . but God giveth it a body". This "bare grain" is divinity potential, which has to be planted in the garden of the world, die and be born again to give God himself — since we are cells in *his* body — a new cycle of conscious existence in this portion of his being.

But, contemplating evolution from the standpoint of the soul's divine origin rather than from that of its earthly situation, Greek philosophy regarded the soul's life here in body as in a very real, though always in a *relative* sense, a veritable "death". In coming to earth the divine spirit exchanged a very high and blessed *potential* life for a very poor *actual* one. It suffered the loss of a whole superior dimension of consciousness. In the realms of disembodiment, consciousness, free of the trammels of the flesh, functions at a level one full degree higher than that which it can experience through the comparatively sluggish instrumentality of the brain. Developed consciousness at that higher level operates with instantaneous rapidity and lucid clarity and vividness.

From this enchanted state it is torn away, "divulsed", as the Greeks put it, from "real being" and sent out into that "far country" of the Prodigal Son allegory. And no minister or theologian has ever told us with authority that that "far country" was this earth of ours. The soul down here is far from its true home in the sense that it is separated from it by a great gap in the scale of vibration rates of consciousness! If gods, angels, men and beasts live in different worlds, even though locally contiguous on the same plane, it is because the grades of consciousness which they severally express are separated from each other as one radio station is separated from another, by differences in frequencies and wavelengths. This, we now know, is the basis of differentiation between the many gradations of conscious life and being. Life ever manifests as or through vibration, and the differences in vibrational character mark the essential diversifications of the numberless forms in life's gradient.

BREAKING THE BREAD OF LIFE

Nowhere do we get the systematic rationale of the situation involving the soul's exchange of heavenly for earthly life so well delineated as in the Greek Orphic and Platonic systems of philosophy. There it is clearly pictured how the soul, when thus "direpted" from her more blissful celestial estate, is carried away into every sort of enfeeblement and diminution of her pristine powers and faculties, the sharp discernment of which can be expressed by English words beginning with "dis-", a prefix that always carries the idea of a scattering of a thing from central unity out into multiplicity, or the *dis*solution of a thing into its component elements. The soul, which by virtue of its possession of higher fourth dimensional consciousness sees things in the spiritual world as units, becomes on its descent to earth blinded to that more complete and perfect vision, a veil being drawn over its "eyes", and, to use the Greek terms, it suffers the *dis*memberment or *dis*mantling of its unitary sight, or its power to see things as wholes. It suffers violent *dis*traction of its focus of consciousness through the *dis*tribution or *dis*semination of its elements, the *dis*persion of its energies in many directions, the *dis*tortion or *dis*turbance of the clarity of its images, the *dis*union and *dis*junction and finally the *dis*cord and *dis*harmony of its whole being attendant upon the loss of its Paradise of loftier consciousness, which then through sorrow, toil and mingled pain and pleasure it must proceed to regain.

This profoundly true and rational basis of Greek philosophy must be restored to its vital place in the edifice of modern theology. The great doctrine of the *dis*memberment and *dis*figurement of the unitary being of deific powers on the upper planes when the Sons of God move outward from center to carry the emanations of divine force forth to material creation, must be reintroduced into the exegetical system, for without these primary principles of knowledge all sound interpretation is impossible. The doctrine has been lost because it appertains to the *in*volutionary arc of the cycle of manifestation, which has been wholly dropped out of consideration through the purblindness that laid all stress upon the *ev*olutionary arc. As St. Paul asks, how can it be that souls have ascended unless they had first descended into the bowels of the earth? If there is to be a resurrection from the "dead", the entity to be resurrected must first have gone down into a grave or tomb of "death".

A philosophy that seeks to rationalize the problems and phenomena of life will hobble along lamely on one foot if it attempts to find solutions by studying evolution while leaving entirely out of view the antecedent process of involution. This observation well enough delineates the prime deficiency of modern scientific rationale in philosophy. Modernity has never once thought to ask — and apply to theology — the simple question: how can you expect a flower stalk in your garden to grow up unless you have first planted its seed there? The whole body of Scriptural truth will continue to grope blindly toward the light of true meaning as long as the antecedent movement of involution is not restored to its place in the dialectical structure of understanding.

All this is extremely pertinent to the present essay because this word "death" is the key word of focal import that carries the whole Biblical reference to the involutionary side of the theological construct. This "death" is precisely what the divine soul suffers upon and through its descent into the human body. It is the comprehensive word used to cover the whole range of the soul's loss of its divine nature or being as it plunges downward on the Jacob's ladder between heaven and earth. It is the Bible testimony and confirmation of the lost doctrine of involution as both a dialectically and a factually necessary precedent of evolution.

If any of the hundreds of students of Greek, Chaldean and Oriental religions who have been conversant with the characterization of the soul's life in body as its "death", has ever caught the idea that possibly the conception could or should be applied to the elucidation of Christian Biblical material, the inkling has never got beyond the recesses of private thought. If at any time the idea generated a hint in this direction, the movement of suggestion that might have gone on to momentous discovery has been discouraged, deterred and thwarted by the instinctive perception of the absolutely shattering and subversive implications which the doctrine held for traditional Christian theology. For the full reach of these involvements embraces the necessary transferal of the "death" of the Son of God from a physical and historical basis and reference to a majestic symbolic depiction of a purely spiritual or anthropological transaction, and that not in the case of one man, but of all men. Christianity is brought face to face with the challenge of an invincible logical thesis, that if the Greek philosophical meaning of "to die" and "the dead" *is* the true intended meaning of these words in the Christian Bible, then the "death" of Christ on the cross can by no legitimate means be circumscribed within the limits of one man's corporeal experience on a wooden cross, but must have its meaning in the experience of the soul on its cross of matter and limitation in every human life.

It would need no elaborated dissertation to limn in all intelligent minds the picture of the inevitable muddle of erroneous meanings that has been produced by the mistaking of the word "death" as referring to the demise of physical bodies instead of the deadened condition of the soul while incarnated in such bodies. So arrant a blunder would not only miss the high meaning intended, but would precipitate the sense over into every kind of anomalous and ludicrous predicament. Precisely this is what it has done in many instances, and it has at all times drawn the minds of millions off the path of true instruction and knowledge and out into a thicket of weird and egregious theological beliefs that have come nigh to unsettling the reason of Occidental nations. The default of knowledge of this one item alone has caused the miscarriage of all religious effort from the sheer fact that because of the mislocation of the realm of "death" the world has been deprived of the good that would have flowed from the realization that all the manifold experiences it has been taught to expect to encounter in the spirit world after bodily decease are its experiences now being undergone on earth. Readily it can be seen that, while looking in the wrong world for the Biblical characterizations of "death", and waiting for this life to terminate before the land of "death" will be entered, Western man has totally missed the vital reference and the gist of all Scriptural meaning that was intended to bear directly upon the crucial significance of the experience he was living through in *this* land of the soul's "death". The confusion consequent upon the theological displacement of the soul's "death" by the body's demise has perpetuated untold and endless befuddlement in all the labors of Christian theology for sixteen centuries.

THROUGH DEATH TO LIFE

Heraclitus, the first philosopher generally mentioned in histories of philosophy, gives expression to a conception which is quite basic for the intelligent approach to this ancient view of the soul's life in body. He speaks of the several elements formed by the gradations of atomic composition of matter at different levels and says that a lower one "lives the death" of a higher one, as a higher one dies under the *life* of a lower one. "Water lives the death of air", he says, as "air lives the death of fire". This is to say that the seed of a higher life must give its vital essence over to a sort of static "death" when it projects its energies outward and downward and incorporates them in organisms existing on the plane below its own status, thus to become the inspiriting, ensouling life-giving principle in those organisms. To give its energic life to a kingdom or entity below it in rank, it must die away or die out to the full conscious expression of being on its own plane. It must in this fashion lose its own life in order to give life to a being below it, which otherwise could not be lifted up to higher kingdom. So it must "die" to redeem the life of the creature below it! Here is the first truly scientific statement of the theological structure underlying Christianity. And it is this purely dialectical principle of understanding that has been grossly travestied into the asserted historical sacrifice of a man on a wooden cross!

If a spark of the divine fire is to enter upon the career of another living expression in renewed cycles, it must, like the vegetable oak, suffer its seed to be planted in the soil of the kingdom immediately below it in the scale. Its descent in seed form to lie buried deep in the soil of the lower stratum of organic growth, is for it obviously to suffer "death", — "until the time appointed" for the recovery of its growth, or its "resurrection". Thus it becomes incontrovertibly clear that the incarnation of life in seed form in the body of a lower kingdom carried with it in ancient philosophical reflection the connotation of a "death". It is equally firmly established, also, that while the soul's condition in this state fully warranted the designation of "death", nevertheless it was to be understood in a relative sense, not as in any way an extinction or annihilation or total end of being for the entity so buried in matter.

Hence it was a "living death" that soul endured in body, or a "death" from which, at the turn round the nadir point of the cycle, there would be inevitably a resurrection. Also it was a "death" which, instead of actual loss, brought immeasurable gain. It was itself the inescapable pathway to higher life. The life that would increase itself in potency and glory must first lose itself. In the light of this enunciation can now be understood the perfectly natural and beneficent meaning of this "hard saying" that has heretofore cast its darksome shadow of apprehension and dread across the pathway to Christian glory.

So we find St. Paul exulting in the sage philosophical asseveration that "for me to die is gain". The Son of God willingly approached the cross of "death" in material embodiment to win heightened glory in the celestial realms, since the generation of brighter glory there is the fruit of the soul's strivings in the life on earth. For "it must needs be that Christ should suffer and enter into his glory". Through the gateway of sin and "death" came also the resurrection from the "dead", as Paul says.

The exposition of this epochal disclosure will be the more solidly grounded if it is introduced with the presentation of a modest selection of excerpts from ancient, particularly Greek, philosophy, to put beyond cavil the use of these cardinal words in the sense, not surely of the body's demise, but of the soul's incarnation. To have mistaken the "death" of the soul *in* body for the decease of the physical life of the body itself, will thus be seen to have been the fatal blunder that wrecked Christian theology.

THE VOICE OF ANCIENT PHILOSOPHY

The conception in its fulness is most frankly expressed in *The Gorgias* of Plato, when Socrates says to Cebes: "For indeed, as you also say, life is a grievous thing. For I should not wonder if Euripides spoke the truth when he says: 'Who knows whether to live is not to die, and to die is not to live?' And perhaps we are in reality dead. For I have heard from one of the wise that we are now dead; and that the body is our sepulcher; but that the part of the soul in which the desires are contained is of such a nature that it can be persuaded and hurled upward and downward".

The intimation here clearly is that Socrates was expounding the position of the conscious entity, the soul or psyche in man, which, standing midway between physical body below and divine spirit above, is capable of being drawn either downward into "death" under the dominance of sensual appetites or upward into heavenly life by the attractions of the beauty of virtue. For Paul tells us that "the interests of the flesh meant death, the interests of the soul meant life and peace".

In the *Enneads* (I, lviii) of the great Plotinus, third century Neo-Platonist, there is found a straight presentment of the conception: "When the soul has descended into generation (from this first divine condition) she partakes of evil and is carried a great way into a state the opposite of her first purity and integrity, to be entirely merged in it . . . and death to her is, while baptized or immersed in the present body, to descend into matter and be wholly subjected to it. This is what is meant by the *falling asleep in Hades* of those who have come there".

Attention should be called in passing to Plotinus' use of the word "baptized" to describe or refer to incarnation. To incarnate was to be plunged into the water of the physical body! This is the true meaning of the baptism in ancient theology. Paul accentuates this idea also most directly when, speaking of Christ, he says that "we suffer *death* with him in his *baptism*", thus identifying death and baptism as the same one experience, and both meaning the incarnation.

To this may be added an excerpt from Pythagoras, who is claimed by many to have been the Greek progenitor of the whole Platonic system: "Whatever we see *when awake is death*; and when asleep a dream". It is a strange thought that, as Socrates expresses it to Cebes, the life we are presumably *living* here may, from the standpoint of more extended consciousness and the reduced dimensionality and reality of the experience, be a form of veritable "death", as compared with the vividness of a life we could live in a world where we would be disencumbered of body and free of its circumscriptions. That we are blindly groping about down here in a wonderland of vague dreams in a state of semi-sleep, missing the grander reality of life and more glorious and blissful vision of true being in supernal states, is not only not a new and bizarre conception limited to the Greek philosophers, but is indeed widely current in reflective poetry and in fact is the presumptive claim of nearly all religions. That heaven is the true home of the soul, and that the latter is astray here in a mournful exile far from its Father's celestial house, is a commonplace idea finding expression in the Prodigal Son allegory and in Christian literature everywhere. It was one of the higher conceptions drawn by early Christianity from the fountains of Greek philosophy.

Perhaps the most discerning and competent of all expositors of Greek philosophy is Thomas Taylor, whose splendid translations and commentaries have been passed over by the academic world in a preference for the far less revealing translations of Jowett. In a dissertation on the Mysteries, Taylor writes that the Greeks "believed that human souls were confined in the body as in a prison, a condition which was denominated genesis or generation; from which Dionysus would liberate them. This generation, which linked the soul to body, was supposed to be a kind of death to the higher form of life. Evil is inherent to this condition, the soul dwelling in the body as in a *prison* or a *grave* . . . The earthly life is a dream rather than a reality . . . The soul is purified and separated from the evils of this condition by knowledge".

This is so typical a presentation of the ground bases of Greek philosophy that it deserves comment. Evil as a cosmic principle has been genetically derived in Greek thought from spirit's association with matter. To spirit dissociated from matter all highest good is attributed. On its own high plane it is altogether pure. It is only through its contact with, imprisonment in and subjection to matter that it is cast down into evil conditions. The segment of Christianity that derived from Gnosticism and Greek sources through Paul carried this strain of thought into all its later theology. It became the root source of the egregious ascetic movement and practices of later centuries of Christian Europe. In the shadow of this view it was accounted as degradation for the soul to be tied to mortal body, and any inclination to let the appetencies and passions of the flesh dominate the immortal spirit was looked upon as horrendous. To subdue and mortify the flesh and seat spirit on the throne of the individual life was the motive of the asceticism that swept early Medieval Christianity like a plague.

For soul to be driven out of heaven and sent down to earth to be "cribbed, cabined and confined" in a vesture of mortal decay was for it a cosmic abasement grievous enough to be theologized as its descent into hell. All Hindu philosophy centered on the soul's struggling to divest itself at the earliest possible moment of its incubus of the body. The soul's life down here was held to be a veritable imprisonment, her wings clipped by the sad diminution of her powers and the limitations imposed on her freedom by the inhibiting sluggishness and inertia of her physical instruments of cognition. To incarnate in fleshly body was for her to suffer the agonies of virtual "death". Only the knowledge of profoundest philosophy, embracing the true science of the soul, would provide men with understanding adequate to orient the mind to endure the carnal nature with equanimity and imperturbability (the *ataraxia* of the Stoics) and to liberate the consciousness from the painful distractions of the sensuous life to the placid contemplation of the more real verities of the spirit.

SPIRITS IN PRISON

Plato himself said that "men are placed in the body as in a prison". He even considered the body as the sepulcher of the soul, an idea that carried one step farther the ancient Egyptian representation of the body, personalized in the Goddess Hathor, as the "bird-cage of the soul". That this imprisonment was equated with the idea of "death" to the soul is clearly expressed by Taylor who, in commenting on the writings of Macrobius, writes: "The soul in the present life may be said to die, as far as it is possible for a soul to die; occultly intimating that the death of the soul was nothing more than a profound union with the ruinous bonds of the body". To impart to the body *its* life by linking to it the soul's more dynamic voltage, nature extracted from the higher principle the plenary quantum of its life to be offered as an oblation for the benefit of the lower order. So the body lived the "death" of soul, and soul died unto the life of the body, as Heraclitus would have put it.

All this is explicitly set forth in apt phraseology by Taylor who, in his *Select Works of Porphyry* says: "What is here said by Plato is beautifully unfolded by Olympiodorus in his MS Commentary on the *Gorgias*, as follows: "Euripides (in *Phryxo*) says that to live is to die, and to die is to live. For the soul, coming hither, as she imparts life to the body, so she partakes through this of a certain privation of life; but this is an evil. When separated, therefore, from the body, she lives in reality; for she *dies here*, through participating in privation of life, because the body becomes the source of evils. And hence it is necessary to subdue the body".

The logic of all this is at least on the face of it unquestionable, unarguable. If the soul is called upon in incarnation to give away its life to the lower organism it certainly cannot retain possession of it for itself. Here we have the ground foundation of the great central arch in the temple of religion known as the sacrificial oblation of the Son of God, who *gave his life* for the world of men. He threw his energic powers into the bodies of mortals so that they might have this connection with a battery of higher dynamism, by drawing upon which they might rise to a higher and more abundant life than as natural creatures they could ever gain without such condescension of the gods. The Sons of God had to give their life and die on the cross of matter, that lower orders might have a visible link with divinity.

So general was this conception among the intelligent in the Greek sphere of culture that the soul's entry into body at the latter's birth was called its *burial*. The Egyptians called it its mummification. In this connection it is likely that the reference of Jesus to his disciples' anointing him for his "burial" can find its true and more meaningful explication in taking his "burial" in its Greek sense as his incarnation in the flesh. We have noted Plotinus's statement that death, to the soul, was to descend under the power of matter and to be subjected to its torpid influences. No less a figure than the great Roman poet Virgil adds his assent to this view: "For souls are deadened by earthly forms and members subject to death".

One needs but recur to the Epistles of St. Paul to find evidence of the great Apostle's accord with this element of Greek philosophy. He speaks of the "law of death" "which is in my members". Flesh and body are at war with soul and spirit. The clamor of the sensuous desires long overwhelms the still small voice of the spirit. A hasty and too simple deduction from all this seemed to dictate the drastic subjugation of the fleshly appetencies and the crucifixion of the body. A doleful chapter of Christian and indeed all other religious history transpired in the wake of this uncritical conclusion.

Again Plato likened the soul's bondage in corporeal existence to the condition of an oyster bound in its shell.

One must note, too, Milton's expression of Adam's surprise, in *Paradise Lost,* when, on being expelled from the Garden of Supernal Paradise for "disobedience" to God's command, with the penalty of "death" pronounced against him for his transgression, he stands, as it were, awaiting the fall of the axe that would terminate his life. But no axe falls; he does not die as he expected. He lives on. If this is the "death" God had threatened for his sin, it turned out to be a living "death". So a new significance flashes into the commonplace Scriptural citation: "In the midst of life we are in death".

It will be indeed a strange and awesome reflection that must accrue from long acquaintance with the lost Greek philosophy that in truth and in fact we are now in the deepest "death" we shall ever experience henceforth in our evolution. We have been in deeper wells and hells of material embodiment in past cycles, no doubt. But as from the present, the bodily life we now lead holds us as deeply in the underworld of physical coarseness as the necessities of our education require, and the future will reward past and present rectitude with better conditions in each ensuing life on earth. This happy assurance is one of those liberating influences by which intelligence frees the soul from the "evils" of residence in body.

As the study of the illuminating Greek philosophy proceeded there was no failure to apprehend the significant role which this singular feature of Hellenic esotericism played in ancient religious systematism. Hundreds of scholars had grasped and familiarly handled the idea in many a work. But always it was treated as a somewhat unique and distinctly characteristic Greek conception. That it might be found to extend its influence beyond the Greek area of speculation and indeed stand in pivotal strategic relation to Western Christian theology and its source-spring, the Christian Bible, was apparently never caught even on the farthest horizons of Occidental reflection. The staggering discovery that the Greek sense of the words did indeed apply to the Bible and theology and that this revelation would transform the house of world religion, illuminating it with a new resplendence, was to come at a later stage of the study.

THE BOOK OF THE DEAD

The hints that prodded speculation on toward the momentous discovery were caught in a field laying outside the area of Greek thought, — the Egyptian. Books of the eminent academic Egyptologists were scanned first, and an introduction was gained into the mysteries of the prodigious lore of the land of Khem. But the orthodox scholastic treatment of the Egyptian books left the mind still shrouded in fog, doing little to dispel the mist from the mystery. Out of much desultory reading in this alcove there came only one sharp suggestion in the direction of the denouement that was to come. This was in connection with the Egyptian name of the so-called Egyptian "Bible", the great *Book of the Dead.* Here was "death" again, and in the very title of the selected compilation of the greatest of the documents found in the Nile valley. The question arose: Did the Egyptians write a Bible to be used only by the spirits of the dead in the after life; a book to be disregarded by living mortals on earth and only to be consulted for guidance in the heaven world following bodily demise? Of what use to mortals could be a book which was written, as Budge had affirmed, "for the use of the dead in all periods of Egyptian history"? To simple reason it seemed illogical that a Bible of a great nation should be written, not for the living, but for the dead (in the ordinary physical sense). It appeared more than chimerical to assume that the overlords and semi-divine guardians of early humanity would indite books of proven wisdom and put them in the hands of the living inhabitants of earth, if the instruction therein was not to be profited by and applied to the present life in which the books were read, but was to be held in abeyance, so to say, until death took the individuals over into another realm of being, where the precepts were to be put into practice. Surely mortals have use for Bibles here, rather than in spirit life. Could a deceased person take his *Book of the Dead* with him and use it as manual for his conduct in the land of spirits! Indubitably a Bible must be meant to appertain to the life of that world in which it was produced and in which it could be read, and to edify the life lived therein.

The Egyptian name of the compilation of fragments called (first by Lepsius) *The Book of the Dead* was *pert em heru,* the translation of which was given as "the Day of Manifestation," or "the Coming Forth by Day". Here was food for thought. This sounded more suggestive of the resurrection than of death. And, sure enough, the very first chapter of the collection dealt with the resurrection. The puzzle deepened. But it was not to find its amazing resolution until some time later.

Good fortune led to the reading of Egyptian lore through the works of the one scholar who, scorned by the scholastics as Thomas Taylor has been, came measurably close to solving the Sphinx riddle of the mighty Egyptian wisdom, — Gerald Massey. His six ponderous tomes were devoured with avidity, as new light shone forth from every page. He missed by very little what all the other investigators had missed *in toto.* He is the only Egyptologist who has come close to descrying what the sage Egyptians were actually talking about under their astute hieroglyphic forms of representation. The others have missed it utterly and tragically.

In the first volume of his <u>*Ancient Egypt, the Light of the World,*</u> at about page 180, Massey, dissertating upon the Platonic doctrine of the soul's regaining its memory lost in its descent into earthly body, or the Doctrine of Reminiscence, asserted that Plato, drawing the teaching from ancient Egypt, "had misapplied it to the past lives and pre-existence of human being dwelling on the earth", when according to Massey, it should properly apply to the soul's memory in heaven of its past earth life following the demise of the body. The soul in heaven, he claimed, would regain the full memory of its (one) life on earth.

To a mind then fresh from the impact of the magnificent conceptions of the Greek systemology and soul science, it was obvious that in this assertion, not Plato, but Massey, had "misapplied" the doctrine. One knew that the great Plato had not blundered in his basic formulations. As the elements of this clash of interpretative ideas were sharply arrayed in the mind, as by some magical light of intuition, there flashed into recognition with blinding splendor a discernment that not only resolved the Massey-Plato conflict in clear outlines, but opened up in one stupendous revelation the whole vision of lost meaning of all ancient religion. The great light spread out to illumine every single doctrine of primal Christianity in its true bearing, for it proved to be the long-lost key to all the Scriptures of the archaic world. It was the open sesame to all constructions, to all exegesis, to all meaning in the Scriptures of antiquity.

It also held the explication of why the Egyptian Bible was called *The Book of the Dead*. For those whom they dubbed "the dead" are ourselves, the living humans. The antique tome of supernal wisdom and transcendent knowledge was after all not, as Budge and all the other beguiled scholastics thought, "written for the benefit of the dead (in their sense) in all periods of Egyptian history", but written, as common logic had insisted they should be, for the benefit of living mortals, whom, however, they regarded philosophically as "the dead". It was seen that there was no clash between Massey and Plato save that Plato was using the word "death" in its esoteric philosophical sense, and Massey was using it in its common reference to bodily decease.

And what was that flash of illumination that came at that one moment of clear insight to unlock the meaning of thousands of volumes hitherto read in befuddlement and confusion of ideas? It was the astounding realization that indeed and in truth, beyond all cavil and controversy, the three pivotal words, "death", "the dead", and "to die" bore the same cryptic meaning and reference in the Christian and Hebrew Scriptures, creeds and theologies as they did in Greek and Egyptian books of old! The lost light of ancient Egypt had been rekindled.

The rush of clarifications of scores of texts, the flood of new and more luminous meaning in every dialectical situation in the theological purview, was an experience never to be forgotten. The light of new comprehension was almost blinding. In its permeating radiance the entire structure of all ancient sagacity stood revealed in all the grandeur of its divine harmony and beauty. Items and features that in the gloom of imperfect understanding had stood athwart the vision mystifying and unrelated to the whole, now were seen in their almost incredible relevance and symmetry. The entire structure, bathed for the first time in a clear light that revealed its full form and majesty, was awesome in its wonder and glory. Hidden in the darkness of the Middle Ages for sixteen hundred years, the temple of ancient wisdom now stood forth flooded with the aura of knowledge that restored its supernal loveliness once more.

CHRIST CRUCIFIED IN EGYPT

First and with almost terrifying force came the certain realization that the central key doctrine of Christianity — the death and resurrection of the Son of God to redeem humanity — could not possibly connote the death of the *body,* the physical demise, of any man-savior, but could bear true meaning only in reference to the soul-death of the Sons of God collectively in their incarnation in all men. At one stroke of sound understanding the historical foundations of apostolic Christianity and its Gospels were swept from under the entire structure. The "death" of the crucified One was seen to be his incarceration in mortal body, not his bloody torture and decease on a cross of wood. That which "died" to rise again was the Christ-soul; and catastrophe had ensued in Christian counsels and Christian history because this "death" of imperishable soul was misconceived to be the physical death of a one-man embodiment of the Christ-spirit.

Along with that came the astounding assurance that the Christ's resurrection could have nothing to do with the rising of a corpse and its bursting the bars of a rock tomb on a Judean hillside on any Easter morn. This was now seen to be allegorism depicting the soul's eventual bursting the gates of this hell of imprisonment in the flesh and winging its way in the glory of celestial light back to its empyrean home, the "sting of death" and the "victory of the grave" having been overcome at the last trump.

Hard on the heels of these overpowering realizations came a startling corroboration of the restored interpretation, one that has strangely survived Christian manhandling of the Scriptural texts, in the eleventh chapter of *Revelation.* If, as five or six Church Councils have decreed in utmost solemnity, every word of the Bible is God's infallible truth, then at least one verse of the Holy Book negates the whole story of the four Gospels, taken historically. The apocalyptic writer (who, say many discerning scholars, could *not* have been the disciple John!) is speaking of the "two witnesses", previously called "the two olive trees", but taken by theology to be two hierarchical powers; and in the preceding verse he says that the "dragon" shall rise up and slay them. Then in verse eight he makes the statement that puts all historical Christianity on the stand for searching cross examination: "And their dead bodies shall lie in the street of the city which is spiritually called Sodom and Egypt, where also our Lord was crucified".

Only the flash of light dimmed for eighteen centuries and reillumined as Massey's *"Egypt"* was being perused, provided a dialectical basis for the salvation of Christianity in its proper essence and message from the devastating implications of that remarkable eighth verse. What! The Lord Christ not crucified in Jerusalem, but in a city *spiritually* named Sodom *and* Egypt! And Egypt not even the name of a geographical earthly city, but of a land and nation! (And even that meaning disqualified by our present knowledge that the name "Egypt" in both Old and *New Testaments* is an allegorical designation for earth itself, the "underworld" into which souls descend for incarnate life!) Also there is the damaging consideration that geographically and historically Sodom and Egypt were not one and the same place, a fact which makes it necessary to assign one crucifixion to two different places, and neither of them the place claimed for the event in the Gospel stories. If the statement in this eighth verse is in any sense true, then it refutes the whole of the Gospel accounts of a physical crucifixion of the man Jesus in Jerusalem. And with characteristic subterfuge the ecclesiastical system of Christianity has evaded the issue presented by the conflict between this verse and the Gospels.

From this precarious dilemma Christian theology can be saved only by the resources provided by the very philosophies which the Church, both early and late, has pronounced heretical. The now readily discernible clue is hidden in the word "spiritually", the adverb used to describe the manner of the naming of the city of the crucifixion. If this locality was "spiritually", (another translation says "mystically") called by several names, it could not have been a geographical town, but must have been a "spiritual" city! One of St. Augustine's two major books, which is indeed one of the foundation pillars of the Christian faith, is entitled *The City of God*; and this, it is to be noted, is no geographical municipality, but clearly a kingdom of spiritual consciousness. So, then, there can be no dispute over the figurative meaning of verse eight, which clearly states that the principle of Christly spirituality is crucified in this lower world, or city of mortal consciousness, and thus only spiritually, not physically, crucified. It was the crucifixion of soul in a physical body, but not the crucifixion *of* a physical body. And that difference represents the vast abyss between sane understanding of Biblical meaning and ghastly misunderstanding in centuries of Christian theology. The death and crucifixion was that of divine soul on the cross of the flesh, and in no sense that of fleshly body on a cross of wood. The latter, however, was used symbolically and dramatically to typify the former, and ignorance mistook it for the actuality in a historical sense. It was soul, not body, that met crucifixion and "death." The mortal body, named variously Sodom and Egypt, *is* itself the cross, on whose four arms the Christ-soul is crucified.

In the view here brought to light with clarifying force it can be seen at one sweep how through the blunder of mistaking the Christ-death for the demise of a bodily personality, instead of the "death" of divine soul when incarnated in all bodies, and entifying the cross as a piece of wood instead of the bodily life and limitations, Christianity has lost the purport of its entire original message for intelligence, has indeed exactly reversed the axis pole of all its organic wholeness and so has almost come to teach the very opposite of what its literature meant to convey. By taking "death" to refer to the decease of physical body (and that of one man alone), and therefore being forced to take the phrase "after death" as pointing to the *post-mortem* spiritual existence in heaven worlds, the meaning-message of Christianity has been shunted clear out of the world in and for which its theology was to have cogent and helpful application, and has landed over in a world of disembodied existence, where its intent was not directly to have reference at any time! By this error in cryptological interpretation [Page 38] Christianity has missed the world for the behoof and uplift of which it was intended, and shot its meaning and reference over into a supernal world where it had no direct or immediate application.

IN THE UNDERWORLD

Then came the further glow of illumination from the new-found meaning of the name of that mysterious world into which all mythological heroes find their way, a world so baffling to savants and scholars through all the many centuries. This elusive region of the myths is the so-called "underworld", or "nether earth". The ancient Egyptian books named it *Amenta*; in the Hebrew Scriptures it is *Sheol*; in the Greek system it is *Hades*; and in Christian theology it is the *Hell* of the creeds. Scholars have been at sea for ages in their effort to localize this lower region of the soul's existence, which it entered at or after "death". Their addiction to the common meaning of the word "death" as the demise of the body kept them searching everlastingly for the locale of this dark realm of the "dead" in every possible area in which the spirits, or "shades" of the dead might be thought to take residence. The more general conclusion among many wild surmises was that it was one of the "lower hells" of the spirit world, some gloomier level of the "astral plane" of the Theosophists. Some were content to let its location rest with the six feet of grave space beneath the sod. Budge, the great Egyptologist, was finally forced to confess that it was neither in heaven nor on earth, but suspended somewhere between the two in an indeterminate region! By some again it was put down in actual subterranean caverns. All the while the scholars, wedded to the idea that it must be a place inhabited by souls after (physical) death, and assuming it could not be rational to think that we were denizens of it at this very time, refused to look for it in the one place where it lay before their eyes at every moment of life, — on earth itself. They could not ever catch the conception that "under" was used in reference to the primal point of life's departure in creation, the heaven world; and so they kept on seeking for it under *this world.* With their failure properly to locate *Amenta,* together with their equal blindness in failing to sense the cryptic meaning of "death" in the Scriptures, they have missed every true connotation of ancient sacred revelation of wisdom and knowledge, and contorted the message of Holy Writ into a ribald hodge-podge of error and idiocy.

In the lucid moment of that flash of understanding it was seen that every meaning in every theological or Scriptural presentment immediately falls into its proper niche in the one grand edifice of religious truth. So clear was this realization that it was obvious that the architectural lineaments of that grand temple never could be beheld in all their harmony and beauty without the clarifying beams of these two lost principia of rationalization. But when, in their light, the structure was viewed in all its integrity, the organic unity of the whole and the interrelation of every part, were equally vivid discernments of transcendent intellectual magnificence. The "lost meaning of death" and the proper location of the "underworld" of mythology were the two crucial keys needed to unlock the ancient casket of "divine theology", and their recovery was certain to transform religion henceforth from its character of a dementia-breeding superstition into its original force for racial salvation. These two emendations would inaugurate a new culture in a new world.

In the ancient day — if Plato's time may be called ancient — the great body of esoteric teaching, conveying to initiated minds these cryptic connotations of basic terms and concepts, was confined to the narrow cycle of the few who could read and attend lectures in the schools of the Mystery Brotherhoods. There was no possibility, hence no thought, of attempting its popularization among the masses. It was necessarily esoteric, the possession of the few literati. Little wonder, therefore, that when the rabid promulgators of Christianity determined to spread their new gospel among the multitude, they ignored and later despised the secret knowledge of the esoteric cultists. This observation is in itself an item that religious scholarship has overlooked. Christianity shortly took the road of appeal to the sympathies, the predilections, the emotions and the ignorance of the downtrodden masses, and thereby closed every door of connection between its popular advertisement of personal salvation and true intellectual understanding and knowledge. Paul, from every indication, endeavored to reestablish the connection and to reintroduce the Gnosis and the Greek esoteric wisdom; whereupon immediately the wing of Petrine, apostolic and "primitive" Christianity vociferously denounced and opposed his efforts. It is a "miracle" of some magnitude indeed that his fifteen Epistles were kept in the ecclesiastical canon at all. As every honest writer has observed, his exposition of "the wisdom hidden in a mystery" has practically nothing whatever to do with the faith and movement assumedly set in motion by Jesus and the Judean disciples and apostles in Palestine.

But now we have reached an age in the development of mankind when it may be possible to disseminate the occult truths to the general populace. Every attempt hitherto has resulted in the direct distortion and falsification of the cryptic presentation, with mostly calamitous historical repercussion. Now, however, the general level of intelligence is perhaps high enough for the release of buried truth with fair hope of no catastrophic consequences.

And it is clear that St. Paul uses the term "death" in the connotation which this brochure assigns to it, as its true meaning in the Scriptures of antiquity. Excerpts from his Epistles will confirm that statement.

It was overwhelmingly thrilling to reflect that the lost secrets of the world's antique literature had found solution again in this modern age, and with involvements and consequences for history henceforth that staggered the mind to anticipate. It is difficult to describe the satisfaction that sprang from the knowledge that the "underworld" of mythology is just this good earth, and that the "dead" of the Scriptures are our own souls flitting about here amid the murky shadows of the images of truth and reality. Broken was the haunting dread of those bogies which a fearful theology had reified in the imagination of sensitive childhood; gone was the fear of a future ordeal of punishment for earthly misdeeds in a fiery hell of torment. For *this life* is the Hades, Sheol and Amenta, and whatever it held of pain and horror was being met now and found not by any means horrific. And there was the positive knowledge, mighty in its comfort and cheer, that if this is the "death" of the soul, it is one that looks ever toward the dawn of a wondrous day of awakening and a final resurrection to a life of ineffable glory. A thousand phantoms of traditional orthodox religious "teaching" were instantaneously dissolved in the sunshine of the intelligence that the Scriptural tomb of death is nothing more fearsome than the physical bodies we wear on earth, and that our bursting the bars of that tomb is nothing more insuperable than the mastery of a truly spiritual science. It was a prodigious gain of peace and serenity when all the unintelligible and irrational collation of theological asseverations that held the mind in a world of doubt and confusion was lucidly resolved into the actualities of conscious evolution in the present life. It was nothing less than a joyous release from morbid unhappiness to know at last that all the spectral experiences promised by current theology for a darkly unknown future were being lived through, and not too unhappily, in the life now running. In a word, the new light removed at one flash of its beams the sting of death.

THE TOMB OF THE BODY

At about the same time there came one of the numberless correlations of meaning that continued to be revealed through the study of comparative philology, one indeed that supplied overwhelming corroboration to the discernment made through the reading of Massey's exegetics. Two English words of four letters each and differing in only one of them were seen to be alike because they esoterically connote the same thing. These two revealing words were "tomb" and "womb". If soul went to its "death" when it entered the body of a child, then that body must be actually its tomb, grave, sarcophagus, sepulcher and mummy case. But since also in that very tomb of "death" it was destined in the course of its cycle to have its rebirth or resurrection from "death", then also this body became in time its "womb" of new life. That vehicle which became its tomb of death, was also the conceiving mother-womb of its new birth!

And this startling correlation from two English words was more than corroborated by a similar, but even stronger kinship of structure that united two Greek words, namely *soma,* body, and *sema,* tomb. There is no escaping the deduction that the Greek Sages saw the body *as* the tomb, as well as the womb of the soul.

Along with the sweeping current of endless new enlightenments that came with every fresh sally of thought from the gate of the new premises there flashed the discernment of the esoteric meaning of the descent into and exodus from "Egypt". Here was another reorientation and clarification of a whole segment of *both Old* and *New Testament* cryptography. The geographical Egypt, lying south and west of Judea, fitted the allegorical direction in which souls from above traveled on their way down to earth and body. They went "west", then "south. . If one will examine the charted direction of Abraham's journeying from the empyrean of heavenly fire, Ur, to "Egypt," it will be found that he went first west, then south.

The Egyptians called the "dead" the "Westerners", those who had "gone west" to "death". A few scholars have been astute enough to see that "Egypt" in the Scriptures cannot be taken as the geographical country of the Nile Valley. To do so turns many texts referring to it into asinine irrelevance. The "Egypt" of the Bible is the allegorical designation for this same "underworld", Hades, Sheol, Amenta, lying "south" (that is below in the sense of inferior gradations of life's power) of the heavenly kingdoms. *We are now in "Egypt",* "the land of bondage", — "that slave pen", as the Moffatt translation of the Bible phrases it. Our diviner spirits are in humble servitude under the power of the elements of the flesh and of the world. They came here to do a work which could not be done in heaven. For this world alone provides the fulcrum of matter against which spirit can base and brace itself to exert its potential might. We are, as souls, being crucified in this world. And so it is no miscarriage of truth when the *Revelation* verse says that Christ was crucified in "Egypt."

Furthermore, in *Old Testament* allegorism, "Egypt" could only be escaped by crossing the "Red Sea". As elaborated elsewhere, the liquid nature of the human body — composed of seven-eighths water — and that red in color, really solves the mystery of the "Red Sea". The soul must pass through its ordeals of living experience in the red fluid of the body to make its final exodus from the "flesh pots of Egypt". At any rate corrected modern translations of the Scriptures have taken the Red Sea out of the text! In Moffatt's translation it has become, and correctly, the "Reed Sea." Literalists must stand dumbfounded at this disappearance of their geographical body of water from the story. Yet, oddly enough, that very phrase, when taken in another and its obviously true sense, brings it back to them as the (physical) body composed mainly as water. Literally enough they must know that they are making their evolutionary way from "Egypt" to "Canaan" through a red body of water — the human blood!

In Greek mythology the god of the underworld was Pluto. He seized Proserpina, the divine soul, daughter of Ceres, cosmic intellect, and dragged her down from the light of day in the upper realms into his darksome kingdom and forced her to marry him. The myth becomes alight with meaning when it is known that the "underworld" is this earth. For the soul is impelled by divine necessity to descend here below and marry the kingly powers that rule it.

In the meaning-glyphs of ancient Egypt Osiris was the Pluto, king of the "dead". Says Massey: "The buried Osiris represented the god in matter". But King Spirit goes into a torpor when first he plunges into this underworld. Matter stupefies his powers and faculties. So Osiris was overcome with stupor and had to be awakened and regenerated by his own son, represented as the Father's own nature, a while "dead", but revived again. So the souls that had entered this nether earth were termed "sleepers in their coffins", "prisoners in their cells", or "spirits in prison". Even the Christian Gospels retain a fringe of this symbolism in their brief statement that during the three days Jesus lay in the tomb of death between his crucifixion and his resurrection he descended into hell and there preached to the "spirits in prison". In the 142nd *Psalm* the soul prays that God will bring it up "out of prison". *Isaiah* (42) says that the people are "snared in holes and they are hid in prison houses". And the same chapter states that the Lord will come into this "underworld" "to open blind eyes, to bring out the prisoners from the prison, and them that sit in darkness out of the prison house".

Matching this in the old Egyptian books we find the soul beseeching its deity: "Imprison not my soul; keep not in custody my shade; let the path be open to my soul; let it not be made captive by those who imprison the shades of the dead." And again it pleads: "Let not Osiris enter into the dungeon of the captives."

Massey clearly sets forth the nature of this "underground" Amenta in his description, so closely matching Christian phrases: "The wilderness of the nether earth, being a land of graves, where the dead awaited the coming of Horus . . . to wake them in their coffins and lead them from this land of darkness to the land of day". (Let it be remembered here that the real title of the Egyptian *Book of the Dead* is "The Coming Forth Into the Day.") How closely this harmonizes with the proclamation of the Christ himself, when he says in the Gospels: "Verily, verily I say unto you, the hour is coming and now is, when *the dead* shall hear the voice of the Son of God; and they that hear shall live. Marvel not at this, for the hour is coming in which all that are in their graves shall hear his voice". And does it need an ornate word picture to paint the mental muddle and its gruesome influences that have been generated by the inveterate error of mistaking these graves of our physical bodies for cemetery holes and marble mausoleums?

And countless millions have read these words with only a vague and uncertain wonder as to what sort of a phenomenon was to occur at some incalculable day of a purely mystical spirit-future; or with the fanatically precipitated conviction that this call to all past dead souls would come within their life-time and on some given date. The deluded Millerites of 1837 set the date for April 17, 1843, and thousands disposed of their property to be disencumbered of worldly goods for the apocalyptic denouement. Some modern groups still come forth from time to time with a proclamation of the date when the elements will consume the planet and bring Scriptural "prophecy" to a head. Yet the globe goes serenely swinging in its circles and doubtless will prove recalcitrant to Bible "prophecy" for some millions of years at least.

It is an instructive exercise to attempt to imagine the difference this one Bible passage alone would have made, or can still make, in the life of the world if the true instead of a false and wholly impossible meaning was read into the words "the dead" and the "grave". Instead of being left pondering in perplexity over a promised planetary and racial debacle and holocaust that is unbelievable on any familiar natural basis and psychologically damaging through its incitement to doubt and fear, the reader would be instantly galvanized into dynamic appreciation of their reference to his own life, not in some ill-defined and speculative state of unnatural existence "in the grave" tied somehow to the last few bones and teeth of his earthly cadaver, but in the living present, when, alive as he assumes he is, he begins to realize that his soul is in an actual torpor of veritable "death" to all the more ecstatic possibilities of expanded consciousness which are potential in his divine part, and that he needs to be here and now awakened out of "the body of this death", as St. Paul names it. Then would come to his mind the realizing sense of Paul's cry to us from the Greek wisdom of two thousand years ago: "Awake, thou that sleepest, and arise from the dead, and Christ will give thee light". "For ye are dead, and your life is hid with Christ in God". "Ye are dead in your trespasses and sins", for "to be carnally minded is death". The Christ himself adds: "You must not let sin have your members for the service of vice; you must dedicate yourselves to God as men who have been brought from death to life".

Back in the Old Testament *Isaiah* had said in the plainest of words: "We live in darkness *like the dead*". And *Job* declares: "I laid me down in death and slept; I awaked; for the

Lord sustaineth me". If the word "death" is taken here in its ordinary sense of bodily demise, it would say that Job had already once died and been brought back to life. As this is not supposable, then the word bears some other connotation than its common one, and it is that of a soul-death. This is a splendid sample of how in hundreds of passages the substitution of the philosophic sense for the exoteric literal one redeems the text from baffling nonsense to rational meaning.

In the forty-ninth *Psalm* it is said that "like sheep they are laid in the grave". Does this mean rows of cemetery graves? Not if one remembers that the figure of a lamb led to the slaughter and to his grave was applied to the Christ himself. In the *Psalms* (49 and 89) and in *Hosea* (13) the spirit of God says that he will redeem "my soul" and "their souls" from the power of the grave and of death. Can this bear logical reference to anything save the freeing of the divine spirit locked up in man's corporeal constitution from its bondage under such limitations?

What nobler consolation and inspiration would have come from the innumerable recitals of the beautiful twenty-third *Psalm* if the proper philosophical sense of "the valley of the shadow of death" had been inculcated in all minds! Even down here in the murks and shadows of "death" which the soul must undergo the God presence attends us, and its rod and staff will guide and support us. It will anoint our heads with the oil of gladness, till our cup of blessing runneth over in sheer plentitude of divine love.

Jonah, plunged down to the very "roots of the mountains" in the depths of the "bowels of the earth", cries up to God: "Out of the belly of hell do I cry unto thee, O God!"

It is pertinent to ask here what point that peculiar sentence in the Gospels could have which says that "the Gospel will be preached to them that are dead" if it does not refer to mortals who, here in living bodies, are yet asleep in soul. (*I Peter* 4; 6.)

But an astonishingly direct and unequivocal allusion to "death" in the Greek sense is found in the first verses of the third chapter of *Revelation*. Could any statement be more explicit? The Moffatt translation has brought out with striking force the straight meaning of the words, which it seems almost evident the Authorized Version has attempted to cover over: "Ye have the name of being alive, but *ye are dead*; wake up, rally what is still left to you, though it is on the very point of death". This ringing call, like Paul's cry to the dead to awake, and arise, is shouted at living people on the earth, yet they are declared to be and are named "the dead". Living people are told to awake from death! And no one in two thousand years caught the inescapable inference that the word "dead" applied to the mortals alive in body, but "dead" in soul. And many a Sabbath School teacher, in answer to some child's query as to how a minister can preach to the dead, has blushingly asserted that this is a reference to the way the deceased Jesus spent his three days in the grave "preaching to the spirits in prison". Inexorably the meaning had to be kept within the aura of the graveyard tombstones.

Anticipating a chorus of rejoinders that the words have been taken in a spiritual sense, alluding to a moral death, and not the sheer physical sense of decease of body, so that the critique here is overdrawn, let it be said that this opens no door of escape from the critical strictures of orthodox position here advanced. Of course there has been intelligence enough to read into the words the sense of a moral-spiritual deadness. But this still fails to catch and carry the implications of the Greek philosophical use of the terms and their full theological import, because moral and spiritual deadness was not connected dialectically with the incarnation. It was left simply to earthly dereliction and depravity. It connotes these, of course, for they come with the earth life. But orthodox conception has never demonstrated any dialectical link between these worldly failings and the soul's plunge into water body.

And how are we to interpret Paul's utterance of almost tragic despair (*Romans* 7:24) other than as an allusion to the soul's stupefaction under its immersion in this fluid body, when in that memorable passage he cries out that he perceives in his members a law which wars against the law of his mind, and ends with the wail of almost moral desperation: "Wretched man that I am, who shall deliver me from the body of *this death*?" And how shall we take his meaning? It is a dubious phrase at best. Does "body" refer to the physical corpus? Or is it a metaphorical figurism for the density and solidity of the soul's "dead" state of consciousness? Any way, how can "death" have a body? Is it a possibility that conniving scribes — as it is confessed they often have done — took a phrase which clearly said "this death (of the soul) *in the body*," and transposed it over into the meaningless "body of this death"? But if it is an uncorrupted text and correctly translated, it is one of the surest and most open namings of this life as "death" in the Bible. It is therefore a notable and memorable passage.

UNDER THE LAW OF SIN AND DEATH

But it is reserved for the seventh chapter of *Romans* (as seen especially in the Moffatt translation) to yield our study the most pointed and amazing corroborations of the interpretative thesis here presented. Paul there (verse five) starts with the assertion that "the sinful cravings excited by the Law were active in our members, and made us *fruitful to death*. But now we are delivered from the Law, being dead to that wherein we were held, that we should serve in newness of spirit, and not under the old code of the letter". Hundreds of exegetical books have utterly missed the inner purport of this vital statement because they have missed the meaning of that term "the Law" by the proverbial thousand miles. They have taken it to be the old Hebraic Mosaic or Levitical moral and spiritual code-laws regulating the physical observance of an endless list of ethical and ceremonial rites, when all the time it is the "law" of the fleshly members, the law of the lower animal nature inclining unto "sin", the law of the sensual life of the physical body, in contradistinction to the higher law of spiritual goodness. The one binds the soul to the body and hence to "death"; the other frees it to the life of spiritual "liberty of the Sons of God".

But what Paul clearly means is that, as he says in *Galatians* (4), "while we were yet children (in the evolutionary sense), not knowing God, we were in bondage to them that by nature are no gods", — meaning the elemental powers dominating the physical body and the world. When at last we grew into the recognition of a higher and diviner law ruling evolution, the law of righteousness, we then "died" unto the influences of the natural law, and we stood out free from its dominance and were reborn in newness of spirit. Just so said the old Greek philosophy.

But the Apostle goes on. Under the natural law we developed "sin", because the tendencies excited by the animal nature, which at first and for a long time is not yet subdued and disciplined by the God-soul, drive us into sensual expression; and for the god in man to behave according to the nature and instincts of the animal in whose body he was for the time a tenant and over whose inclinations he had covenanted to act as king and lord, was to commit "sin". And as "sin" could be overcome and "died unto" only by additional experience of incarnational "death" for the soul thus recreant to its covenanted vows, the Apostle rightly tells us that "by sin came death". Surely this consequence followed the indulgence in animality, since that bound the soul still longer to animal body, imprisonment in which is a living "death".

But then Paul extends the chain of theological dialectic by unfolding its next link. If "by sin came death", then by death "came also the resurrection from the dead". For the pain suffered by the soul in consequence of its "sinful" life of transgression would eventually bring an end to the sinning and a final escape — so much insisted upon in Hindu philosophy — from the round of birth and death in the body.

Then Paul gives expression to perhaps the most positive affirmation that his allusion to "death" is to be taken in its full Greek philosophical sweep and sense, when he makes the extraordinary statements which follow: "I lived at one time without Law myself; but when the command came home to me, sin sprang to life and I died; the command that meant *life* proved *death* to me. The command gave an impulse to sin, sin beguiled me and used the command to *kill* me. So the Law at any rate is holy, the command is holy, just and for our good".

It is doubtful if there is any more pregnant passage in the Scriptures than this for both overt and covert mental illumination of the fundamental principles of Christian theology. It needs comment and analysis.

What does Paul mean by saying that he lived at one time without Law himself? It cannot mean that he had lived a life of pure spiritual goodness in the present incarnation, for he elsewhere expressly bemoans his failure and error. So it must refer to his spiritual existence in the upper heavens before his soul's descent to earth. In the upper world his soul had enjoyed the *liberty* of the Sons of God. Surely in heaven there is no sin, and no law of the members to goad to sin — since there are no "members". The animal below man and the angels above him are both without sin; only man is "born in sin". Paul himself certifies this conclusion when in the very first verse of that same chapter he writes: "Know ye not, brethren (for I speak to them that know the law,) how that the law hath dominion over a man as long as he liveth?" Would we not be warranted in asserting that he meant to say "only as long as a man liveth?" This would be simply to say that he meant us to understand that the law applies to souls in earth, not to spirits in heaven. Every religion in the world has virtually based its message of consolation to mortals enduring the hardships of this life on the assurance that return to heaven at life's end would release the soul from all earthly bondage. The point in Paul's mind is just a reminder of the obvious truth that in incarnation the soul comes under the law that governs earthly bodies, from which it is free in the supernal worlds. That theologians have mistaken this "law" for Jewish religious rigor instead of simply the law of the flesh exercising dominion over the soul when soul has entered its domain, is surely one of the most arrant instances of mental aberration in all the history of religious thought.

But then comes a word which has never received a single true interpretation to give the wonderful philosophy of the passage a chance to be caught by minds starving for truth. It is the "command". The soul in the empyrean is without Law and without sin. But there comes to it a "command". And this "command" is going to break in upon and end its celestial serenity and blessedness, and plunge it into sin. What can so direful a thing as this be? What is this "command"?

Be it noted, then, for the first time in ages, it is the command which comes to all embryonic souls in the cosmic heavens to end their dreamy placidity of supernal consciousness and come down to earth or some other star. *It is the command to incarnate!*

Failure to catch the crucially significant meaning of this one word has been due to the fact that in the authorized version of the New Testament, whether designedly or through ignorance, the word has been mistranslated "commandment" instead of "command". From the context no one could possibly determine what this "commandment" referred to;

there is not a clue given; the apostle has not mentioned any "commandment", actually none is in sight anywhere in the situation under discussion. The use of the word leaves the passage in blank incomprehension and meaninglessness. It is well known that the exegesis of Paul's theological elucidations in this *Epistle to the Romans* has perplexed and baffled orthodox scholarship beyond any other portion of the New Testament. It is obviously all due to the failure to grasp the reference of these two words, the "law" and the "command", along with, of course, that lost Greek connotation of the word "death".

And when this command comes home to the soul above and draws it into its downward plunge, as all archaic writings agree, "sin springs to life", and the soul marches on down the Jacob's ladder to enter the cycle of its "death", "burial" and "resurrection" in the earthly body! For the soul in its descent, or involution, abandons its life of spiritual blissfulness in purely subjective states and comes by successive stages closer, closer to the flesh, which, through its sinful cravings excited by the Law of the carnal consciousness, will blot out its memory of diviner motions of the spirit and overwhelm it with the coarser motivations of sense life. The nearer it comes to full submergence in the body the deeper is its coma of "death" to all its higher sensibilities, and the greater its bent to "sin". Its approach to the flesh gives "sin" its chance to "spring to life" in a mode or height of consciousness not hitherto subject to such a spur. The full plunge into the "moist nature" of the body completes the soul's "death" on the cross of matter.

So the divine command, which meant a new chance at life, and life more abundant than ever achievable by the soul before, through the opportunity of a new experience of growth in the mastery of the elements of all worlds, — the command that "meant (more) life" proved "death" unto the soul, as Paul says. Here is new light sufficient to regenerate the decadent life of Christianity. This is the ancient saving truth of life regained after long centuries of hallucinated blindness.

And it is notable that the Apostle ends his dissertation with the final conclusion that all this sin and death of soul in body is NOT the evil thing that ages of wretched miscalculation have pictured it in all the generations of Christian history. Was this descent of soul into earthly body its sinful "fall", its disobedience to God's command? At last the common miscarriage of the allegory in *Genesis* is refuted by Paul's clear exegesis. Man's descent to earth was NOT in disobedience to God's command, but in full compliance with it. God's command brought the soul to earth. "Man's first disobedience", as Milton puts it, was NOT a wrecking of God's command or of his plan for his human children. Aiming a rejoinder at what were doubtless current misunderstandings and misrepresentations of the allegories in his own day, Paul asks: "Did what was meant for my good prove fatal to me?" And it is as if he concentrates a thousand "No's" and "God forbids'" in his smashing answer to all this theological stupidity. "Never!" shouts the Apostle; and that "Never!" should go echoing about the earth and swirl within the inner precincts of all philosophical and theological brains from now on. For it is the crushing refutation of all the theologies of Adam's sin, involving all humanity in one man's dereliction, the erroneous ideas of man's "fall", and the whole fallacious scheme of the gruesome and morbid theology of "sin".

Never, shouts Saint Paul, was the descent of the soul into body a fall into sin in any sense of a miscarriage of divine beneficence and divine design. It was God's own planting of the seeds of his own life in their proper soil for a new growth into higher levels of eternal life. Paul ends by saying that the springing to life of sin and the resultant "death" proved beneficent "by *making use* of this *good* thing". The whole incarnational process, that takes the soul through the valley of the shadow of sin and death, is "this *good* thing", for which the Apostle says the whole cycle of existence is ordained.

Only in esoteric circles of the present has it been recognized that the Prodigal Son story in the *New Testament* is a beautiful allegory of the soul's descent into animal body, its long forgetfulness of its diviner home above, its awakening to that memory and its valiant resolve to return thither up the ladder of evolution. It was one of the parables or Logia of the Lord, uttered by the character taking the role of the Christos in the Mystery dramatizations of old. Only in the purview of the meaning elucidated here can the Father's rebuke of the elder brother's churlish reluctance to welcome back the returned wastrel, and his statement of the ground of his rejoicing, be dialectically rationalized. For the Father says: "This my Son was *dead,* and is alive again". And since he was alive in the human sense the while he was wasting his substance in riotous living and feeding on the husks that the swine did eat, the Father's assertion that he was "dead" can have no other meaning than that he was alive on earth, but with his soul groveling in its "death" under the gross motivations inspired by the fleshly lusts.

In *Luke* (20:38) it is stated that the Supreme Deity "is not the God of the dead, but of the living, for all men live unto him". Several approaches to the likely meaning are open; but it seems plain that the most obvious one is to take it that the God presence in man, through his Son, or Sons, is not an active and vital power for those in whose nature the immanent principle of Christliness is not yet aroused to function, but that it is an active saving leaven for those who have come alive and awake to its working power, who have become the "living" from the "dead", through having implemented the hidden potency of divine mind.

TO HIM THAT OVERCOMETH

A strange phraseology is found in Egyptian and other literature that is closely related to this theme of the soul's "death" in body and which touches the fringe of Christian theology, in which, however, it has never received noticeable emphasis. It has to do with what is called "the second death". After noting its occurrence prominently in Egyptian scripts, one was surprised to find it directly in the Christian canon also. In the *Book of Revelation* one of the seven promises made to "him that overcometh" is that "he shall not suffer the second death". This cannot well be apprehended in its true bearing unless the significance of the first "death" is also correctly envisaged. The naive intellect has had to wonder what a *second* death can mean to a mortal, to whom his own (Christian) Scriptures aver that "it is given unto man *once* to die". If a man dies as a mortal, how can he die again? As a spirit? But all religion distinctly affirms that it is precisely as a spirit that death *cannot* reach him. A second death in any sense of demise or even of moral decay is not understandable for mankind. The only light of rational diegesis is through the door of the Greek exoteric sense of the soul's "death" as here projected into theology. What, then, can be its meaning?

As *Revelation* has already declared that, while we have the name of being alive, we are in reality "dead", and follows this with the urgent call to us to "Wake up; rally what is still left to us, though it is on the very point of death", it is clear that, already deep in one "death", we are close to the possibility and threat of still another and deeper one. If a Biblical passage warns people already "dead" that they are on the very point of "death", there must be a first "death" and also a second. As there are two births, there are also two "deaths."

We have the grounds of explication before us in our theme. In the philosophy of the age in which the Scriptures were "written" the soul had entered the realm of "death" when it was brought down from heaven and linked to carnal body. This was its first "death". There it lay in "death" until the turn of the cycle brought its awakening and its eventual resurrection from the "dead" condition.

Now, however, if it sank so deeply into the enmired consciousness of the bodily life and the animal nature as to lose the power to awake and arise out of that lethal stupor, and continued to sink further down to a point where its recall "out of Egypt" was impossible (a conceived eventuality in ancient Christological science), it lost its link of attachment to the upper world and its chance to return thither. In that sad case it would suffer the "second death". And, is it strange, then, that this was the only one of the two that was wholesomely dreaded by the Manes (or shades of the "dead" in the underworld) of the Egyptian books? When this danger had been definitely passed at the turn of the cycle, the soul gives vivid expression to its joy at its presumptive salvation from the worst of its ordeals. "I have not suffered the second death", it jubilates. "I have passed the gates of the Tuat", or underworld. "I have successfully passed the most dangerous crisis", it might have cried in modern terms. But the Christian Scriptures closely match the Egyptian meanings. In *Isaiah* it is again the divine soul buried in the first "death" that piteously pleads with the Father that "thou wilt not suffer thine holy one to see corruption; thou wilt show me the path of life" back to the upper levels of Paradise regained. How close this is to the soul's similar cry in Egyptian scrolls: "I shall not putrefy, I shall not rot, I shall not become worms; I shall germinate, I shall live again", each phrase thrice repeated to accentuate the ineffable joyousness.

Proclus, the last of the great Neo-Platonists, warns that the soul must avail itself of the evolutionary opportunities provided by its linkage to flesh "without merging itself too deeply in the darkness of body".

In *I Samuel* (2:6) it is written that "the Eternal kills; the Eternal life bestows; he lowers to death and he lifts up". If comment is not by now superfluous, what sobering reflections should be generated in the minds of intelligent readers by the caught sense of the difference it would have made to all theology if such a passage had been read with the cryptic sense of the Eternal's "killing" us and then "lifting" us up again firmly fixed in all minds, instead of taking it as somehow meaning his actually killing us in the earthly sense. It is not a general item even of theological knowledge that the Eternal is represented as having tried to "kill" every one of the Biblical heroes who, at his command, journeyed down into "Egypt". It is notable in the case of Moses. Even the Jesus of the Gospels had to be assured of his safety in his "flight into Egypt." Paul says the command *"killed"* him and that he "died". (Yet he was a living man, writing of his own "death!") What peculiar brand of death is it that a living man can describe as his own past experience? Let Christian theology answer; let it face the issue it has, through ignorance or chicanery, dodged for two millennia. For its positive answer is central and vital to the intellectual sanity of the millions of its adherents today, and through these, to the possible salvation of the race.

Says *Job:* "I shall die in my nest, and I shall multiply my days like the eagle", or phoenix, the fabled bird of death and resurrection. How can death in its physical sense multiply one's days, obviously on earth? Death ends one's days, it does not multiply them. But in its sense of incarnation each additional "death" and burial in (living) body surely does multiply for the soul not only days, but years and ages of ever more thrilling life.

Let us place alongside of *Job's* rhapsodical utterance one from the *Book of the Dead*. There the soul, in a ritualistic pronouncement that, when philosophically apprehended in all the length and breadth of its cosmic significance, generates almost a transport of exalted feeling, says, as if in a veritable struggle to suppress bursting rapture: "I die, and I am born again, and I renew myself and I grow young each day". And he enlarges on this by exclaiming in climactic ecstasy: "Eternity and everlastingness is my name." Notable it is that the soul's cry of blissful salvation begins with "I shall die". That its prospective "death" is not foreseen as the cause of gloom or sorrow, but the first step in his journey to ineffable expansion of life, proves that the "death" in contemplation is not the thing of evil hap and the end of existence.

One of the most striking evidences of the presence of the lost sense of the word "death" in the Bible, and apparently a tell-tale evidence of the effort of early scribes to suppress the esoteric intent of much of the Scriptures' original text (mishandling of which has been freely admitted), is to be found in verse nine of the famous fifty-third chapter of *Isaiah,* called by theologians "the Chapter of the Suffering Servant". There we find the verse running in the ordinary Bible as follows: "And he hath made his grave with the wicked and with the rich in his *death"*. A marginal note is frank enough to tell us something that opens the door to a most engaging surmise, in view of the issue involved. It states that this final word "death" was in the original Hebrew manuscripts *in the plural number*! It read: ". . . in his deaths". Would it ever occur to ordinary readers what insidious motive might have inspired ancient translators to change this key word from plural to singular? Hardly. Yet it stares one in the face with glaring suggestion of theological duplicity. Surely it is not difficult to envision the natural difficulty a semi-instructed scribe — much more a totally ignorant one — would have in seeing how the word "death" can have any rational meaning whatever in the plural number, seeing that we die but once, — on orthodox doctrinal presuppositions. It could be that some such copyist or theologian, meeting the plural form of the word and finding it hard to reconcile with sensible meaning, ended by figuring it was a mistake, and summarily "corrected" it by substituting the singular form. This is at least a charitable view of the possibilities to account for the change.

But another is possible. Astuter theological discernment, seeing with dismay (after the third century) that the plural number of the word "death" would naturally betray its esoteric and only rational meaning of *multiple incarnations,* deemed it a holy subterfuge to remove all possibility of this calamity by making it singular.

For in Christian theology physical death can have no plural. It must be some other "death" that can be pluralized. And this was doubtless known to the few remaining esotericists in the Christian movement after the debacle of ignorance in the third century, who saw that the verse would give away the then discarded doctrine of reincarnation. Church polity had already decreed the ousting of this too Pagan conception from formulated dogmas. The tell-tale verse had to be made innocuous. "Death" had to be kept singular.

But all too clearly the lucid import of the plural form shines out. "Deaths" could mean only repeated incarnations! In one life the soul made its "grave" (of body) with or among or in low and wicked people; in another it was cast with the rich and the high of the earth. Hindu philosophy gives expression to this very conception. In Sir Edwin Arnold's *The Light of Asia* it is intimated that the entity that comes in one life as a beggar "will come again a king". Here in Christian Scriptures, pronounced to be true in every word and syllable, was the too obvious reference to incarnation as reincarnation. It dared not be permitted to stand. It had to be concealed. The change to the singular did it.

Then there is that perplexing statement in the Scriptures that "the last enemy to be overcome is death". This, taken of course in its assumed meaning of bodily decease, has led uncritical and credulous minds to the weird expectation of an immortality for the human being in the flesh. But this is not in the order or plan of nature. The physical is to have no organic immortality. Flesh and blood cannot inherit the kingdom of heaven.

What, then, it is challenged, is the meaning? Simply that there will be an end to the series of "deaths", meaning incarnations, when the long course of experience in fleshly embodiments on earth is finished and the soul becomes a pillar in the mansions of divinity "to go no more out" into mundane life in this cycle of cosmic evolution. This is surely the overcoming of the last "enemy" of the soul's advance. "Death" will be swallowed up in the soul's crowning and consummative victory in the last incarnation of the series.

The soul's residence in the "darkness" of body being symbolized as its "night-time", and the body's watery composition earning it the allegorical designation as the "sea", luminous clarification of vivid meaning flashes into the mind when one contemplates the *Revelation* assertion that at the day of evolutionary consummation, when the soul has won the victory over the lower elements and returned to spiritual heavens, "there shall be no more *night* and no more *sea*".

It is instructive to compare two passages, one from Egyptian literature and the other from the third chapter of *Revelation*. In both what is to be noticed is a sequence of three states, namely life, to begin with, then death, and after that life again. This is most revealing, as showing the eternal swing of the pendulum between life and "death." First the Egyptian verse. Says the soul in the script of the *Ritual*: "He hath given me the beautiful Amenta (the underworld — this earth) through which the *living* pass from *death* to *life*". And in *Revelation* the Logos proclaims: "I am he that *liveth* and was *dead;* and behold I am *alive* for evermore", Life, "death" and life again forever alternate in the cycles of the soul's eternal journeying.

Empedocles speaks of the cycles of generation. They he says, cause "the living to pass into the dead".

And so it comes to that climactic utterance of the divine soul of man, perhaps the most exultant outburst of holy rapture expressed in the Scriptures. It is from Paul's immortal chapter on the Resurrection, the fifteenth of *First Corinthians.* As the essay concludes with its unforgettable rhapsody, the reader should take it deep into his own inner consciousness as being the glad cry that will go ringing out from his and our own lips as, finally triumphant over our last "enemies" of sense and body, we shall go winging our way verily on pinions of ecstasy back to the celestial home.

"So when this corruptible shall have put on incorruption, and this mortal shall have put on immortality, then shall be brought to pass the saying that is written:

Death is swallowed up of victory.
O grave, where is thy victory?
O death, where is thy sting?

The End.